LITTLE BIBLE
JEWELS TO AMAZE

Ronda Hastings

John 3:16

LITTLE BIBLE JEWELS TO AMAZE

By Ronda Hastings

Illustrated by Sandy Waggoner

Two-Lane Publishing

Guthrie, Oklahoma

Printed in the United States of America

ISBN-13: 978-1505875683
ISBN-10: 1505875684

Dedication

To my childhood Sunday School teacher, Mrs. Lora Motsinger, who faithfully taught the Word of God and planted biblical seeds within my heart.

"Train up a child in the way he should go: and when he is old, he will not depart from it." **Proverbs 22:6 KJV**

Acknowledgement

A very special thank you to my husband for his encouragement, and our four precious granddaughters who affectionately listen to their Nana's stories. Thanks to my publisher, Two-Lane Publishing, and gratitude to Sandy Waggoner for the illustrations. Much thanks to Trinity Baptist Church at Big Spring, TX for the food purse.

Contents

Little Bible Jewels To Amaze

How to use the lesson guide:

Copy pictures and dialogue pages to use together as a flash card lesson, read the stories aloud using the illustrations as visuals, or can be used as a reading book.
However you choose to use this lesson guide, it was written to inspire your imagination.

Ronda

LITTLE BIBLE
JEWELS TO AMAZE

LEFTOVERS

Li (Lee) stood in front of his new teacher, her proper name was Mrs. Waggoner, but the children affectionately called her Miss Sandy. Lee and his family had immigrated to Kansas from China, on the other side of the world, from the United States.

Lee looked at all the students staring back at him. He was so different from the other children, with his jet black hair, and brown eyes. His family's arrival was not going to be easy for anyone residing in this small Midwestern town.

Lee's first morning at school had gone well, and it was soon time for everyone to file out to the cafeteria to assemble for lunch. Lee would not be buying the school lunch so the teacher in charge that day instructed him to take a place at the table, while the other students waited to purchase their meal.

Standing in line together were four of his classmates: Raymond Hess, Brandon Smith, Donald Meech, and Cory

Blankinship. Those boys were a handful, and Miss Sandy was experiencing her share of difficulty with them this year. The four boys kept peeking over at Lee, laughing and talking as they waited for their pizza. They continued pointing and whispering while heading over to their regular table in the corner, eating their lunches before going back to class.

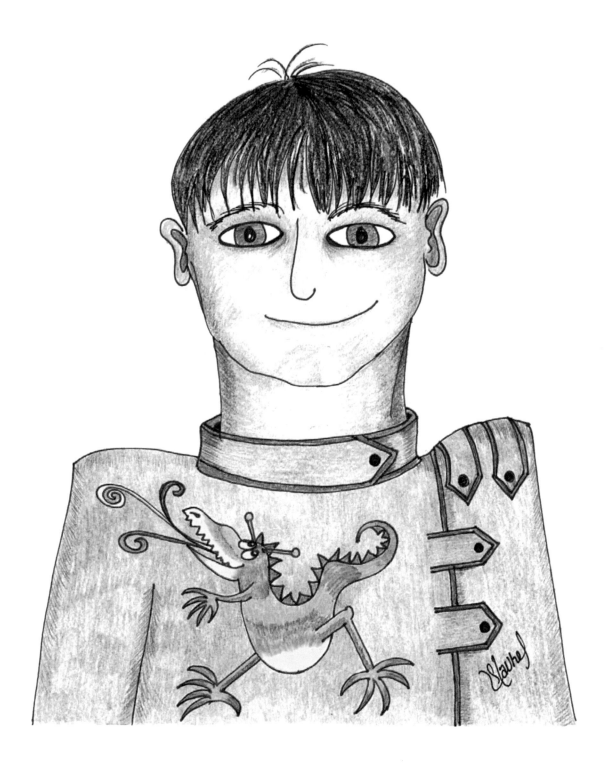

Lee enjoyed school, even though he was having a hard time making any friends. Aware that all the other students just put up with him, he was not worried, knowing that it would take time for him to be accepted as part of the class. Each lunch period he would sit by himself, eating and watching as the other children walked past his table.

Today, Miss Sandy was scheduled for lunch duty, standing over in the corner, keeping an eye on things. Lee sat at his usual place. He rested his lunch bag on the table. It was kind of a strange looking container with handles, but it made Lee feel at home because it had come with him from China. He removed his rice and vegetables and began to eat his lunch, using his chopsticks.

This day in particular the group of four boys had been extremely bad in their behavior. Miss Sandy had to get on to them numerous times. Raymond winked at Brandon, as they picked up their food. Cory and Donald were right behind the other two. Instead of walking straight over to their table, the boys made a detour to where Lee was seated, laughing as they stood beside him.

Raymond, picking up the container asked, "What is this, a food purse?" Amid, taunts and jeers, Cory took his slice of pizza and moved it back and forth under Lee's nose, and then he took a huge bite, with Raymond uttering, "This is what we eat for lunch, not leftovers." The entire group of students were staring and watching the four boys, as they walked away to their private table and sat down.

Miss Sandy could not believe what she had just witnessed, feeling a flush come across her face. She had never been more disappointed with any of her students, in all of her years as a teacher. Thinking to herself, those boys know better, have they not listened to anything I have been teaching them here at school or in my Sunday School class? Determining right then and there, a special lesson would be taught this coming Sunday for sure.

Early Sunday morning, Mrs. Waggoner arrived at church and prepared for her class, she took an extra amount of time in prayer. She arranged the chairs in her classroom to form a half circle with Raymond, Brandon, Donald, and Cory seated directly in front of her. She attached all her student's names to the chairs that morning, placing every student where she wanted them to sit. Today's Bible lesson would be of special interest to the four boys seated in the middle.

Beginning her class time in prayer, Mrs. Waggoner instructed her students to turn in their Bibles to Matthew, Chapter 14, verses 14 - 21.

"Cory could you please read verse 14?" Miss Sandy asked.

"Sure thing," Cory said and began, "And Jesus went forth, and saw a great multitude, and was moved with compassion toward them, and he healed their sick."

Their teacher explained that the Bible had very clearly stated that Jesus had compassion (concern) toward the people, helping those who were sick.

Raymond was asked to read verses 15, 16, and 17, "And when it was evening, his disciples came to him, saying, This is a desert place, and the time is now past; send the multitude away, that they may go into the villages, and buy themselves victuals [food]. But Jesus said unto them, "They need not depart; give ye them to eat." And they say unto him, "We have here but five loaves, and two fishes."

Setting the stage for the lesson, Mrs. Waggoner illustrating that Jesus had been teaching all day, it was getting late and the people would need to leave to go get something to eat. Jesus had said to his disciples. Why should they travel all the way to the villages to get food? Feed them here. The disciples replying to Jesus, "we have but only five loaves and two fishes."

(Imagine a large group of people and only a small amount of food, how is that going to work?) One of Jesus disciples, Andrew, Simon Peter's brother, saith unto him, "There is a lad here, which hath five barley loaves, and two small fishes: but what are they among so many?"

Asking her students, "to picture in their mind" this boy's mother, aware that he would be traveling to hear Jesus speak, knowing that he would get hungry sometime during the day, as young boys do, she placed food in a satchel for him to carry with him. "Possibly a bag that had handles so he could drape it over his shoulder as he walked." (It might be neat if she had borrowed Lee's bag as an illustration just for those boys. :-))

"Brandon, please read verses 18, 19, and 20," said Miss Sandy. Brandon began, "He said, 'Bring them hither to me.' And he commanded the multitude to sit down on the grass, and took the five loaves, and the two fishes, and looking up to heaven, he blessed, and brake, and gave the loaves to his disciples, and the disciples to the multitude. And they did all eat, and were filled; and they took up of the fragments that remained twelve baskets full." Again their teacher, explaining that all the people seated, were able to eat until they were full.

They didn't just get a small piece of bread and fish, they were able to eat until they could eat no more. There was enough food to feed all the people, and then the disciple's collected twelve baskets of what was left. Donald read verse 21, "And they that had eaten were about five thousand men, beside women and children."

After all the scriptures had been read, a recap of the story was given, explaining that Jesus first had compassion on the people, being kind, giving of Himself, making these strangers feel welcome.

Miss Sandy said, "Jesus did not know this crowd of people, many of them had traveled long distances, they did not all speak the same language, look the same in their appearance, or practice the same customs. Jesus was not unkind because they were different, but loving as He ministered to them. The young boy, also a stranger, shared his meal with the people. He could have been selfish and kept it all to himself, taking pieces of the bread or fish, showing off what he had to eat. When the miracle was complete, the disciples picked up twelve baskets of leftovers. God had supplied food for the disciples (his special men) to share among themselves. Think of what an honor it would have been to partake of God's leftovers," Miss Sandy concluded.

As the students exited her classroom that day, their teacher prayed that God would touch each of their hearts in a special way.

The next day at school, Miss Sandy decided to stand over in the corner of the lunch room, out of sight. Locating Lee sitting at his table, all alone as usual, Raymond, Brandon, Donald, and Cory, entered the room walking directly over to their classmate. Brandon sat down on one side, Raymond on the other, Donald and Cory across from him.

Each boy placed a food purse on the table, removing their leftovers as they started to chat. This time, they included their new friend in the conversation. Miss Sandy, felt tears forming in her eyes. She had never been more proud with any of her students, especially these four boys.

Ephesians 4:32 "And be ye kind one to another, tenderhearted, forgiving one another, even as God for Christ's sake hath forgiven you."

BOSSY BESSY

Bessy roamed the grasslands and walked carefully over the many rocks that were always in the way, keeping well away from the sheep and goats. Bessy had a bad habit of talking, talking all the time. She could never put her mouth in silent mode. The other animals nicknamed her Bossy Bessy because she was so cantankerous -- that's a big word for ANGRY.

Yes, Bessy was not a very happy cow, always worried about what she did not have, and bugging everyone. No one was able to escape her chitchat, blab, blab, this and blab, blab that, and talking non-stop until finally the animals would just have to say "excuse me" and hurry away. All the other cows were careful to peek around the corner of the building where Mrs. Noah did her milking each day. To make certain that Bessy was not around, anyone catching sight of her would tip toe on all four of their hooves and high tail it out of there.

Mr. and Mrs. Noah did not have time to round up the cows and bring them in to be milked every day, so their son, Japheth decided to build a pen to keep all the cattle together.

"Oh my gosh, we are going to have to listen to Bessy all night," complained Gertie.

"I don't think I can stand it," mooed Carrie, "even an hour with Bessy is too much. I'll probably give out purple milk in the morning."

"Oh I can't believe you said that," laughed Hazel, "surely we can act like we are asleep that should fool her."

"No, that will not work," Carrie answered, and sure enough, Bessy chattered all night.

"Did you know that Noah is building an ark? What does he need with an ark, and what is an ark anyway? I have never seen one, have you ever seen one?"

Hazel tried to answer, but Bessy kept right on talking.

"Noah is foolish, working day after day on that silly thing, wasting all his money. If I had that kind of money I would not be spending it on a boat, ark, whatever he calls it. I cannot believe

Mrs. Noah, their sons, and daughters-in-law are helping him. Yesterday, Hamish came over to where they were all working and Noah told him to be prepared because God had delivered a message."

"And, behold, I, even I, do bring a flood of waters upon the earth, to destroy all flesh, wherein is the breath of life, from under heaven; and everything that is in the earth shall die."

"Now that is just crazy, we all know water comes to the earth by a mist, making the grass green and tasting ever so yummy. I do not want to tattle, but Hamish just shook his head and walked away muttering to himself about poor old Noah."

Early in the morning, just as the sun was rising in the East, Carrie and Hazel, thinking that Bessy had fallen asleep, talked about how much fun it would be to go inside the ark with Noah and his family. Bessy butted right into their conversation, (even cows know it's rude and bad manners to talk when someone else is speaking.)

"Now you girls can't possibly be thinking about going aboard that awful looking thing," exclaimed Bessy. "I would never set a hoof upon something as odd as that, and you don't even know how long he will keep you locked up in there. What will you eat? I'd rather graze upon the green grass and drink the fresh water, plus you have to put up with all those other animals. In particular, sheep and goats, demanding the best blades of grass. They'd eat it completely to the ground, greedy, selfish pigs. Acting like they are so much better than anyone else, snobs!" Bessy trotted off with her behind wiggling and her tail smacking flies.

Carrie stuck out her long tongue and crossed her eyes. "I would gladly get on the ark just to get away from that old cow."

"Me too," laughed Hazel.

Bessy spent the entire day spying on the family, sneaking around and listening to everything they had to say. That night she had some more juicy gossip to share with the girls.

"Noah told his family, just a few more weeks of work, and then it would be time to load the ark with provisions. Provisions?"

Carrie spoke as quickly as she could. "Water, barley, seeds, fruits, vegetables, and things like that."

"Well, I never heard of such utter nonsense. Just awful, all that money and provisions thrown away. Water is never going to come down from the sky, why should it? Just because Noah said it is going too? FAIRY TALES! People are making fun of our master and laughing behind his back, saying terrible things about him. Tomorrow, I am going to wander off and see what is over the hill."

Gertie whispered to Carrie and Hazel, "Maybe she will stay; we couldn't be that lucky, could we?"

It was a quiet afternoon, silence filled the air, no one missed the chatterbox, but Bessy was back before dinner, and no one escaped her report.

"The grass was so much nicer on the hill. Green and thick and no sheep or goats to bother with. The water was cool and clear," she had so enjoyed her adventure, but Bessy said it was probably best if they all stayed where they were.

Noah and his family finished the ark quicker than Bessy had predicted. They gathered the provisions and placed everything they would need for their trip in the ark. God directed the animals, birds, every living thing upon the earth that He had chosen, to board the vessel. Hazel, Gertie, and Carrie were among the cows that stepped in through the huge door.

"WOW!" They said as they looked around and saw all the creatures and the inside of the large vessel that they would be living on for months to come.

Bessy, went looking everywhere for the girls, but no one had seen them. She walked over to the ark yelling out so everyone could hear, "Are you in there, Carrie, Hazel, and Gertie? I just bet you are, you silly girls. I am going to wander over the hill and you can just stay here. Don't come crying to me when this is all over and you need a friend."

After seven days, as everyone waited patiently in the ark, God shut the door. Bessy was at her new home, eating the most tender blades of grass, and resting as she chewed her cud. Feeling very pleased about having the lifestyle she had always dreamed about, while her friends were held captive in that ridiculous boat.

Suddenly, droplets of water began to fall from the sky. Bessy didn't know what to say, she was at a loss for words. She had never felt rain before and the wet spots hitting her body made her shiver. The moisture did not stop for days, weeks, months, and before long Bessy was cold and tired of the rain.

The water from under the ground rose higher and higher, causing her to crawl up the tall hill, but still the water kept coming. Bessy, began to remember Noah's words, thinking to herself, "Maybe, I should have talked less and listened more." Bessy had spent too much of her time trying to be the center of attention, consumed with the pleasures of this sinful world. Noah tried to warn her about the danger that was coming, but Bessy couldn't stop talking long enough to listen. When the time came for God to send rain, Bessy was left outside the safety of the ark.

Do you listen to God's word, your parents, Pastor or Sunday School teacher?

Hebrews 13:5 "Let your conversation be without covetousness; and be content with such things as ye have; for he hath said, I will never leave thee, nor forsake thee."

James 1:19 "Wherefore, my beloved brethren, let every man be swift to hear, slow to speak, slow to wrath:"

Psalm 46:1 "God Is our refuge and strength, a very present help in trouble."

JASPER

Crisp morning air greeted the sun, rising over the city of Samaria. Four eggs lay safely in their nests; Onyx would be the first to hatch, next, Ruby arrived, and Jasper was last.

Jasper whispering to himself, "What is this? Not in my nest."

Pushing and pushing until the fourth, tiny, blue-brown speckled egg crashed to the ground.

"Such a naughty raven, really I am," he said as he displayed an evil little smile on his face.

Onyx, Ruby and Jasper were BFF's. Three ravens who spent each day practicing their flying skills, playing jokes on one another, and watching the world below from the sky above. Today they would soar over the palace, setting high upon the hill overlooking the rest of the city.

King Ahab and his wife, Queen Jezebel, were evil in the sight of God. Jezebel was a follower of Baal (her false God) and building shrines (places to worship her false God.) The Bible states that there was never anyone like Ahab, giving himself to evil, helped by his wife.

Queen Jezebel worried too much about her appearance, never satisfied with the way she looked. She dressed in the most beautiful, purple gowns, lining her eyes with the blackest shade of eyeliner, and painting her lids with blue shadow. She powdered her face with white dust, her cheeks and lips painted with the brightest color of red. She showed off her ankle bracelets, toe rings, and the gold crown, covered with jewels every time she stepped out into the public.

The Queen's favorite treasure was her Egyptian cat, Sakmet. Sakmet displayed a sleek, smooth bronze-colored body all covered with dark spots. Her forehead was set off by a birthmark in the shape of the letter M.

Jasper had so much fun being cruel to Sakmet. Diving at her head, and dropping pieces of sticky garbage unto her fur. Today he had a special surprise, rotten fish.

"Such a naughty raven, really I am," he cawed to himself as he flew away.

Sakmet's green eyes glared at Jasper as he floated through the sky.

"One day, I will take my revenge," she meowed, "one day!"

King Ahab sent for Elijah. Elijah did not want to go to the palace, but God had given His prophet a message to deliver to the King. The three bird friends watched as Elijah walked into the courtyard. Jasper, always taking advantage of any excuse to cause trouble, began to dive toward the prophet without any warning.

"Take this old man," he chirped, flying so close to Elijah's head that he made him lose his balance and fall to the ground.

Watching all the drama from the window, King Ahab, began to laugh at the top of his lungs at the sight before him. Queen Jezebel appeared tickled with the mischief that the little raven had caused upon the great Man of God.

Elijah carefully lifted himself from the ground and pointed his staff toward the heavens, "Be sure your sin will find you out," he said before going on into the palace. His statement was directed toward Jasper.

Ahab was still chuckling when Elijah was being presented before the throne, to speak the words God had placed in his mouth, and instructed him to deliver to the King.

"As the Lord God of Israel liveth, before whom I stand, there shall not be dew nor rain these years, but according to my word," said Elijah.

"So it is not going to rain, aye," mocked Ahab. "Who are you, Elijah, to dictate to me, the King, what the sky will do? Get out of my sight and take your silly predictions with you."

God directed Elijah to leave the palace and to hide by the Brook Cherith, where the prophet was placed into the safety of his

Master's hands. Ravens were used to supply the needs of Elijah. Onyx, Ruby and Jasper had been chosen to provide the meals to keep Elijah alive. Onyx, and Ruby seemed eager to help, but Jasper just turned his back and flew away.

"No! I am not going to work my feathers to the bone for that old man," he muttered to himself as he flew back to town.

Onyx and Ruby would take bread and meat to Elijah for breakfast and dinner. Elijah had very little, no fancy clothes like the Queen; he only had a coat made of wool, with a leather belt wrapped around his waist. God supplied all his needs, as only God can do.

It was a long flight for Onyx and Ruby twice a day. The exercise kept them in shape, and they were honored to obey God's commands. While his two friends were busy, Jasper lingered around the city still having his daily pranks with Sakmet, his favorite source of recreation.

Jasper had discovered a huge supply of snacks; items so tasty and delicious. He didn't even have to share. Outside the Temple of Baal lay pieces of meat offered on the altar -- lamb, dove, oxen, and a smorgasbord of other tasty morsels. Each day Jasper would pig out on the goodies left behind, his tummy bursting as he leaned back against the wall. He used his pin feather to pick out the pieces of food stuck between his teeth.

"What fun I have. Onyx and Ruby, working all day and me with nothing to do," said Jasper. "Silly ravens, things could have been so different for them, too bad."

Months hurried by and the brook finally went dry. God directed Elijah to another place to live, allowing Onyx and Ruby to return home. Jasper was shocked to lay eyes on his BFF's. Oh, how they had changed. They were slim, muscular, and glowing from being in presence of God. Jasper chattered about all the things that had happened during their absence. He told them about Sakmet, his new discovery, and on and on he went

"Tomorrow I will share with you my new found abundance," Jasper bragged. "Meet me at the Temple of Baal, at ten o'clock sharp."

Behind the temple, next door to the palace, Jasper pointed out the most delightful portions of meat and bread. Onyx and Ruby had no intention of even touching one piece of the unclean reward, excusing themselves as they left Jasper to indulge alone.

He ate until he was so full he could barely move, and then he reclined in his favored spot. Jasper was pleased with himself, wondering if it might be time to find a new group of friends. Onyx and Ruby were not the same; they had changed, too goody good. Jasper decided he wanted friends more like himself. He closed his eyes and daydreamed of tomorrow's feast.

Jasper listened to the sounds of the city. He heard the sound of a bell in the distance, a chime similar to Sakmet's bell ringing out each time he had played his dirty tricks upon her. Yes, he had been mean to Sakmet, but he didn't have to worry because she was safely locked away inside the walls of the courtyard, with no means of escape.

Visions of food, food, food, whirled around in Japer's head as he accidentally let out a huge burp. He opened one eye and peeked to see if anyone had noticed. Jasper's eyes almost popped out of their sockets when he noticed something slinking around the corner. Standing right in front of him was Sakmet. *How had she slipped away from the palace?*

Jasper began to tremble with fear trying to get on his feet, but his body was too plump to lift himself off the ground. At that moment, his best friends appeared, pulling and pushing trying to get Jasper into the air.

No matter how hard they worked, Jasper could not lift himself off the ground as Sakmet inched closer to her victim. Onyx and Ruby were forced to fly away to safety leaving Jasper to face his punishment alone. Sakmet voiced a happy meow with an evil little smile upon her face and a feather poking out of her lips.

Numbers 32:23 "But if ye will not do so, behold, ye have sinned against the Lord: and be sure your sin will find you out."

Jasper disobeyed God and suffered for his lack of obedience. King Ahab and Queen Jezebel paid the penalty for their sin also. Elijah was protected by God. He performed a miracle in front of the Jewish people and the nation of Israel repented.

TALLIE'S MISADVENTURE

Way out in the West, all by themselves on the hot desert sand, lived a family of tumbleweeds. Now, tumbleweeds come in all shapes and sizes; they are tiny, small, medium, large, and extra large. Tallie's family was made up of every size possible. Great granddad was extra, extra large and he pretty well ran things, having been around for a long time.

Watching a lot of tumbleweeds come and go during his life out on the arid (dry) land called home. Tallie was not the smallest member, but not the biggest either, just somewhere in the middle. She had seen other relatives leave, but each time someone left they would never return.

"What kind of adventure were they having and where had they gone?" Were just some of the questions whirling around in her

mind. Nana tenderly stating, "There is no need to worry about things you don't understand. Just be happy to stay here with your family."

"What is the fun in that," Tallie told nana. "I want danger, thrill, and adventure; it's too boring around here."

Each day as the sun lowered over the mesa (a flat-topped mountain) showing off the most beautiful colors of brown, orange, and red, Tallie would dream. She dreamed about an escape into the big, wide world.

The season of spring in the desert always brought with it strong winds, sometimes blowing so hard and for so long everyone thought it would never stop. The family held on so tightly to one another during those storms that it actually hurt Tallie's hands. Always putting the smallest tumbleweeds in the center, layering by size until the larger members formed the outside of the circle. Great granddad would place himself in the direction of the strongest gales. However, Tallie had decided she no longer needed the protection of her family, inching closer and closer to the outside of the circle.

No one even noticed the undersized tumbleweed at the very edge of the group. Today the wind had been stronger than usual, blowing dust into their eyes, making them sore and itchy. Tallie dropped her hand for just a second to remove a grain of sand, and before she could grab a hold of her cousin, Jake, the wind blew so hard that it lifted Tallie into the air.

Hearing her family begging for her to come back, but sadly she was gone. It was as if someone had let go of a balloon as it drifted up into the sky, higher and higher and then all of a sudden the object took off like a plane flying through the air.

"I've never had so much fun in all my life," Tallie cried out, floating and gliding until the wind began to drop and Tallie hit the ground with a thud.

"Where am I?" Our traveler had landed on a patch of ground not far from the edge of a mesa. The last big gust of wind for the day pushed Tallie over and over along the sand, faster and faster until finally stopping near a big rock.

"Well, here I am and I'd better be happy about it, cause that's where I'm a staying for the night." With the setting of the sun, darkness arrived and Tallie had never been alone at night before. All kinds of strange noises came from everywhere, the wind as it howled through the rocks made a frightful cry. The screech of a bat as it flew past her head, prairie dogs barking in the distance. A group of beetles clicking as they walked across the sand, and the one thing Tallie feared more than anything else coming out of the

darkness. The sound of danger, one she knew too well as it inched closer and closer. A rattlesnake slithered up and placed itself near her bottom.

"Oh! Maybe this wasn't such a good idea after all!" Tallie would have to spend the entire night staying awake to keep from disturbing the sleeping snake, his snore (hiss-rattle-rattle) echoing throughout the canyon. Finally, with the afternoon heat the unwelcome visitor wiggled away.

"Thank goodness. I thought he would never leave. Now what am I going to do?"

That was a good question with no answer.

All evening Tallie sat and worried if the rattlesnake would return, also scolding herself for not paying closer attention to her Nana's words. Darkness brought with it another sleepless night. A tarantula (giant spider) with eight hairy legs, ran back and forth between the tumbleweed and the rock.

As the morning approached with the sun rising in the eastern sky, a little owl landed near Tallie's shoulder. *"Shoo, shoo, go away,"* Tallie cried until she saw old Forked Tongue (the snake) hanging from his beak. She named her hero, Oscar; no special reason she just liked it. That night the coyotes sang out to the moon as it rose into the sky, big and round. Something about a full moon sent all the creatures in the desert into hyperdrive with lizards, mice, and scorpions dancing in the moonlight trying to escape Oscar's sharp claws. This new home had brought about a lot of changes; gone were the days when Tallie could joke with her cousins, listen to Pop's stories, and spend time with the family. Danger, thrill, and adventure were nothing like she had imagined.

Months passed by and Tallie was getting fed up with just sitting near that big rock. She was looking forward to Oscar's visit each morning, missing him during the night as he hunted for food, returning to his perch to spend the day in silence. The songs from the coyotes were starting to annoy her, the same chorus every night; at least they could have changed the tune. No, she was not happy with her new life. *"I have to get away from here, but how?"*

A few weeks later, one afternoon, clouds began to form in the sky above. Turning black and blue as the storm grew bigger, flashes of lightning hitting the ground, when suddenly the winds begin to blow as the rain poured down upon the earth. Oh, what a relief, I am moving again, and so she was. Tallie rolled across the wet sand so quickly that it was impossible to recover from the previous tumble, traveling for miles before coming to a sudden stop. Too dizzy to notice where she was for a few minutes, lying at the side of a small building, looking around, spotting a pen containing a flock of sheep. *"Where there are sheep, there are people,"* Tallie told herself.

About that time a young Navajo boy came out of the small hogan (home) heading over to check on the flock; it was his job to make sure they had all come through the storm unharmed. Not a single ewe or lamb had been hurt in anyway other than being a bit wet. The boy would check on them again each morning. There Tallie rested against the side of the wet building, catching her breath, and grateful to be still in one piece, although she had been bumped and bruised.

The next morning Tallie heard someone coming outside, it was the boy she had noticed the night before, his mother called him *"Hastiin"* (man). He spent a lot of time outside with his sheep. Tallie would see him laying out food, pouring water into the trough, holding the lambs, and petting the ewe's each day. She looked forward to watching him perform his duties and listening to him read from something called a book. Hastiin would read aloud to his younger sister, *"Doli"* (bluebird). Today's reading contained words of great importance.

Hastiin told his sister the story was found in Luke 15:11-24. It would be a long reading, but Doli loved to hear her brother speak, so she sat quietly as he read -- "And he said, A certain man had two sons: And the younger of them said to *his* father, Father, give me the portion of goods that falleth *to me.* And he divided unto them *his* living. And not many days after the younger son gathered all together, and took his journey into a far country, and there wasted his substance with riotous living. And when he had spent all, there arose a mighty famine in that land; and he began to be in want. And he went and joined himself to a citizen of that country; and he sent him into his fields to feed swine. And he would fain have filled his belly with the husks that the swine did eat: and no man gave unto him. And when he came to himself, he said, How many hired servants of my father's have bread enough and to spare, and I perish with hunger! I will arise and go to my father, and will say unto him, Father, I have sinned against heaven, and before thee, And am no more worthy to be called thy son: make me as one of thy hired servants. And he arose, and came to his father. But when he was yet a great way off, his father saw him, and had compassion, and ran, and fell on his neck, and kissed him. And the son said unto him, Father, I have sinned against heaven, and in thy sight, and am no more worthy to be called thy son. But the father said to his servants, Bring forth the best robe, and put *it* on him; and put a ring on his hand, and shoes on *his* feet: And bring hither the fatted calf, and kill *it;* and let us eat, and be merry: For this my son was dead, and is alive again; he was lost, and is found. And they began to be merry."

Tallie lowered her eyes as Hastiin read the story of how this man's son had left his home, looking for things he did not need, just as she had done. If she could only do things over, she would have never moved from the protection of the center of the circle or let go of Jake's hand. Alas, she could not change what had taken place, but maybe there was a reason why she was here. Tallie continued to watch Hastiin each day and listen to the words he spoke, learning that the book he was reading was called the Bible.

One night when the moon was shining very dimly, Tallie noticed something that was not normally near the sheep -- it was a fox. Papa fox had three kits (babies) back in the den and he needed to provide a meal for them to enjoy. Very quietly the fox began to look through the fence picking out the newest lambs. It would be easy to grab one of the defenseless objects and carry it home. Now to find a hole where he could squeeze through. Tallie began to pray, having seen Hastiin and Doli do that many times during her stay here.

"Dear God, I ask for Your help, please send me to the spot where I need to be."

Tallie felt a breeze began to blow her to the far end of the property, where she was pushed into the only hole in the fence. Papa fox tried several times to get through the tumbleweed, but the little thorns Tallie had on her body kept the intruder from getting into the pen. Forcing the fox whose nose was sore and bleeding to return home empty-handed. Tallie was shaking, such a close call, but the little lambs were safe.

The next morning Hastiin found a tumbleweed caught in the fence *"what are you doing here?"* He also noticed some red fur lying on the ground, wondering and shaking his head; Hastiin pulled and pulled until Tallie had been released from the place where she had been trapped all night. Carrying her over the hill, he placed her among a large number of tumbleweeds huddled against the side of a mountain.

"Is that you, Tallie?" a voice cried out. *"Jake?"* Tallie asked. *"I'm home,"* she exclaimed. Before anyone could say another word Tallie pushed her way into the center of the circle, to stay there for a very long time. Tallie would never leave her home again, but one day she would share her adventure with granddaughters of her own.

AUGGIE THE ANCHOR

It had been a long hard day for Quintus, the blacksmith. He had worked well into the evening. He'd spent all afternoon making a new anchor. He hit and stretched the piece of metal, sweating and complaining as he worked. Large flames shot out of the top of the chimney. The fierce heat needed to melt the ore, made the whole building feel hot and sticky. When Quintus finished the anchor, he stood back and admired his work. It was a perfect creation made by his own hands.

(It might be fun to have the boys and girls stand with their arms stretched out at their sides, pretending to resemble an anchor.)

Percy, Quintus' nephew, stayed behind to tidy up the blacksmith's shop. Percy put all of his uncle's tools in their proper places. His final task was to extinguish the fire in the furnace.

These chores had taken much more time than Percy expected. He realized he'd better hurry or his mother would be angry for him being late to dinner. Slamming the door closed, Percy ran down the street to arrive home just as the food was being placed on the table. Percy was unaware that by shutting the door so violently, he had caused the newly made anchor to rattle on the shelf above the work table. Shaking and shaking until all of a sudden, the anchor crashed onto the floor below.

"Ouch! Oh that hurts! I need a band-aid!" cried Auggie the anchor.

One of his arms was bent and twisted. He was in a terrible mess, all alone, and with no one to help him.

The next morning when Quintus and Percy arrived for work, they noticed an object lying in the dirt. Quintus picked Auggie up from the floor, dusted him off, and looked at the damage.

"Oh, this is not good," yelled Quintus, "what happened? All my hard work, gone, destroyed. Well, nothing to do but throw this away. No one will ever want to buy an anchor that is not perfect; something that is useless."

Percy felt terrible about causing the accident, knowing it was his fault.

"I'm sorry," Percy told his uncle.

Then he placed the anchor on a shelf in the back of the building. Auggie, would have to spend weeks and months, covered in cob webs until one day a fisherman came into the shop. The customer was looking around, and noticed something over in the corner.

"What have I found?" he said lifting a strange looking object into the air. "An anchor, how much money are you asking for it? I could use it on my boat."

Quintus was busy and not wanting to be bothered, shouted out, "Awe, it's just an old piece of metal. I'd forgotten all about it. It's not good for anything. Just take it, so I can be rid of it."

That is exactly what the fisherman did. He carried the anchor back to his boat that was sitting in the water. He laid the piece of metal in the sand, taking time to fasten a rope around Auggie, before dropping him into the cold water. Down, down, down, the little anchor drifted until he finally hit the sand below him.

"Whoa! I thought I was never going to stop falling," said Auggie. "So this is what water feels like. AWESOME! I have waited my whole life to be out on the sea."

Many times, Auggie was lifted from the water and placed into the boat, carefully being inspected and checked to be sure that the rope was fastened securely, and then he'd be dropped back down into the sea.

My fisherman has taken very good care of me, Auggie thought. *He is always making sure I am clean and spotless. He picks off pieces of algae (weeds) that stick to my body, and he is cautious to tie the rope in a strong knot. I don't want to be left at the bottom of the sea.* Auggie told himself. Sometimes, Auggie ended up next to the catch of fish, so stinky and yucky.

One night when the boat had drifted far away from the shore, "plop," went Auggie into the water once again. Auggie loved to sit in the sand, although he was just a little afraid of the darkness that surrounded him. Tonight, the moon light shone upon the water like a mirror that reflected the light in Auggie's direction.

He loved that type of night, when the water was still and quiet. Suddenly, while out on the calm sea, a great storm came rushing in and there was no time to get back to shore. The waves began to roll and the water began to whirl, like when you put chocolate into milk and stir it around with a spoon.

"Oh no, I've just been splattered by an octopus, with eight arms going in every direction, trying to grab a hold of me. Let go," shouted Auggie. "I mean it, you had better, get OFF of me!"

Long strings of seaweed, and all types of creepy things with beady eyes came crashing up against Auggie, and the sand beneath him began to move in all directions.

"I'm, Seeeeeeeeeeeea sick, ugh," cried Auggie.

Far above, on the surface of the water, the fishermen were not doing so well either. Huge waves were coming over the sides of the boat; the wind was blowing so strongly, that it almost pushed the men into the water, forcing them to throw everything they owned overboard, keeping only the nets and the oars.

Deep under the sea, Auggie was beginning to lose his grip. He was holding on as tightly to the sand as he could. Now Auggie understood why Quintus, the blacksmith, had wanted rid of him. Auggie was damaged, useless. His friends were in trouble. He needed to try as hard as he could to keep the boat steady. Struggling and struggling, he was working harder than he had ever worked before. He realized only a miracle could save them now. Just when Auggie had given up all hope, he felt his body being lifted and placed onto the boat.

The fishermen were rowing toward the shore. Their arms and bodies were tired and weak. Salty water was splashing everywhere making it hard to see what was before them. Out of the waves, a shadow appeared like a man. Auggie could not believe what was standing before him. *People do not walk on water,* Auggie thought. He watched the spirit coming closer to the boat. The men became afraid. Auggie began to shake, and hid himself under the nets!

A tender voice, came out of the darkness, "It is I; be not afraid."

The men recognized His voice immediately. Peter cried out "It is Jesus."

The Apostles helped the Son of God into the boat and in the blink of an eye, they were all safely upon the shore.

Auggie, had not known the men who took care of him were called "The Apostles." Many times sitting over in the corner in the blacksmith's shop, he had overheard Percy mention Jesus.

Quintus had been unkind with his words concerning Jesus. Auggie knew all too well that words could be cruel. Quintus had said terrible and ugly things about the little anchor, words that were very hurtful, but Auggie had learned a very important lesson.

The happy little anchor didn't have to be perfect to do what he was created to do. He only needed to be willing to use his talents and abilities.

After the Apostles' boat had been repaired, a new rope was attached to Auggie. He was once again ready to ride the wild seas again. This time, knowing God would be watching over him and his fishermen.

Hebrews 6:19 "Which hope we have as an anchor of the soul, both sure and stedfast."

The Bible is like an anchor. If we read and obey God's words, they will keep us safe and secure.

INDEX

A

Abundance - a large amount
Affectionately - show love
Anchor - a heavy object that is dropped from a boat
Apostles - followers of Jesus
Ark – boat

B

Beady - tiny, round
Blacksmith - a person who works with metal
Bothered – troubled

C

Cautious - careful
Cawing - the cry of a raven
Compassion - a feeling of wanting to help
Complaining - to make known unhappy feelings
Consumed - to waste
Conversation - talk, how you behave
Covetousness - greed
Crisp - clear and cool
Cud - food
Customs – habit

D

Den - the home of wild animals
Depart - go away
Destroyed – broken

E

Ewe - a female sheep
Extinguishing - put out

INDEX

F

Fain - happy
Famine - not enough food to eat
Fastened - close
Fierce - strong
Flock - a group of sheep
Flush - turn red
Fragments - broken pieces
Furnace - hot oven

G

Gales - a very strong wind
Graze – eat

H

Hooves - feet
Huddled - to come close together in a group
Husks – thin dry layer of plant material that cover seeds and fruits

I

Illustrating - explain
Inspected - to look at
Intruder - come or go where you are not wanted

J

Journey - traveling from one place to another

M

Miracle - a wonderful event
Multitude - large group

N

Numerous – many

INDEX

O

Obstacle - an object that blocks your way
Ore – rock

P

Perform - to do
Predictions - an event that is told about before it happens
Provisions - a supply of food

R

Raven - a large shiny blackbird
Realizing - to get
Refuge - protection from danger
Residing – live
Revenge - to get even
Ridiculous - laughable
Riotous - exciting, fun

S

Scolding - blaming
Securely - make safe
Slithered - to move like a snake
Sockets - where the eyes are set
Spirit - ghost
Substance - things, property
Swine – pigs

T

Trotted - walk
Trough - a container from which animals drink

ABOUT THE AUTHOR

Ronda Blevins Hastings is a wife, mother, mother-in-law, and grandmother to four delightful granddaughters.

Ronda grew up near Hume, Missouri, and Fort Scott, Kansas. Sheltered among family and friends, where she was taught to appreciate and love the land that was so cherished by these small farming communities.

While attending Fort Scott Community College, Ronda's teacher, Mrs. Lucile James introduced her to the art of writing, a craft that would be put on the back burner as Ronda's life branched out into a different direction.

In 1982, God opened the door for the Hastings family to serve Him in the South Pacific nation of New Zealand. Ronda and her husband, Brad, spent twenty-five precious years living and ministering among the people of Auckland and the capital city of Wellington.

Since 2008, Ronda has resided in the quaint town of Grants, New Mexico, assisting her husband at the Faith Baptist Mission located on old Route 66, admiring and working among the Native American people living on the Haystack and Baca Reservations.

This lifestyle change has provided the unique opportunity for Ronda to pursue her passion for writing and gardening. Life in the desert has inspired several of her stories; the mesas as they rise up from the earth, tumble weeds as they scurry across the barren land and the sounds of ravens as they fly through the endless, blue skies.

Ronda may be reached at Ronda2nz@hotmail.com
www.facebook.com/AuthorRondaHastings